Rawmarsh St. Joseph's
Catholic Primary School

Little People, **BIG DREAMS**
AMELIA EARHART

Written by
Mª Isabel Sánchez Vegara

Illustrated by
Mariadiamantes

Translated by Raquel Plitt

Frances Lincoln
Children's Books

When Amelia was a little girl, she liked to imagine she could stretch her wings and fly like a bird.

When she was older, she went to an air show.
The planes soared into the sky, leaving Amelia
on the ground. She wished she could go with
them and see what they saw.

She got a ride in an aeroplane and liked it so much she didn't want to ever come down.

So Amelia learnt to fly. After months of practising, she became the first woman to fly up to 14,000 feet.

With a mechanic and a pilot, she was also the first
woman to try and fly over the enormous Atlantic ocean.
As they set off, she waved at whales far beneath her.

After many hours, they reached land.
The world looked small, so small.
The houses and cars were like toys.

Even though Amelia wasn't flying the plane,
when they landed she became famous. People
around the world were inspired by her story.

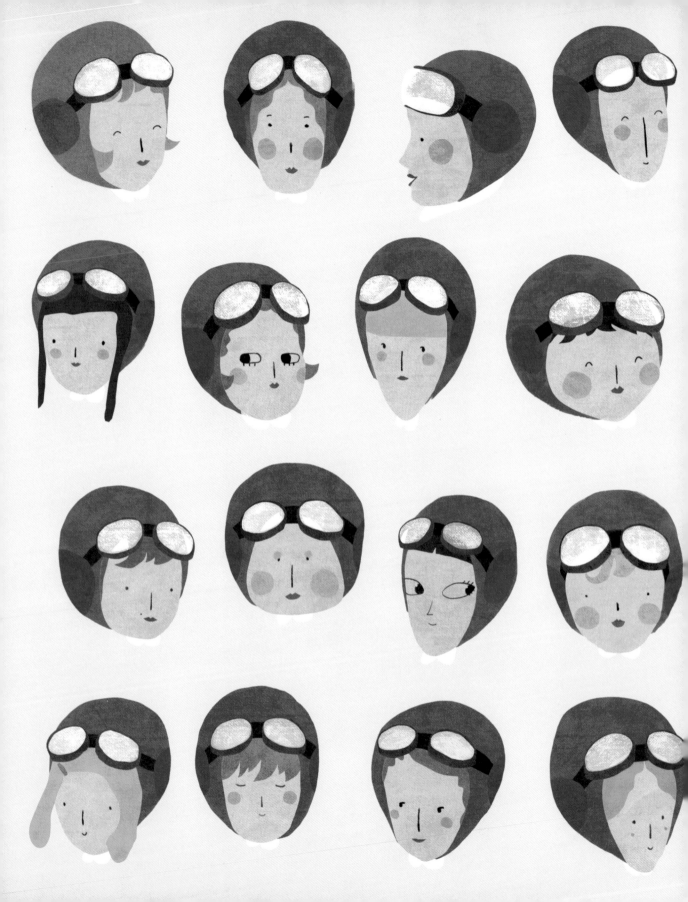

Amelia thought that every girl deserved to fly,
so she founded a club with 98 other fearless pilots.
A little later, she flew across the Atlantic all by herself.

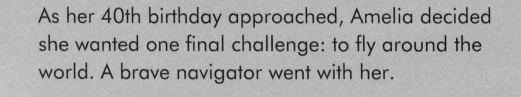

As her 40th birthday approached, Amelia decided she wanted one final challenge: to fly around the world. A brave navigator went with her.

They flew for thousands of miles,
over oceans and jungles...

... and over the savannah, where giraffes turned their heads in their trail. Some people said the journey was crazy.

But Amelia wasn't afraid of living a thousand adventures. So she flew on like a bird, further than anyone had gone before…

... never to return.

Because Amelia always followed her own advice:
"If you want to do something, do it."

You never know how far you could get!

AMELIA EARHART

(Born 1897 • Disappeared 1937)

1904

1928

Amelia Earhart was the most famous female pilot of the
twentieth century. She first became interested in planes after
seeing an air show when she was nearly twenty years old. A
little later, pilot Frank Hawks gave her a ride in a biplane. From
that moment on, she said, "I knew I had to fly". Amelia took
lessons and bought her first plane six months later. She used
it to set a new women's world record by flying up to 14,000
feet. She was the first woman to fly over the Atlantic, first with a
mechanic and a pilot, and later by herself. In 1929, Amelia was
the first president of the Ninety-Nines, an organisation that

1932   1937

supported female pilots. In 1935, she became the first person
to fly solo across the Pacific Ocean. But Amelia was always
keen for a new challenge. In 1937, she decided to try and
fly around the world, a total of 29,000 miles. On July 2, she
was trying to reach Howland Island in the mid-Pacific when
she reported that their gas was running low. Soon after, all
communications from the plane stopped. There was a massive
rescue attempt, but Amelia and her plane had vanished.
In 1938, a lighthouse was built on Howland Island in her
memory, and today her bravery is celebrated around the world.

Want to find out more about **Amelia Earhart**?
Have a read of these great books:

Who Was Amelia Earhart? by Kate Boehm Jerome and David Cain
I Am Amelia Earhart by Brad Meltzer and Christopher Eliopoulos
Amelia Earhart: The Legend of the Lost Aviator by Shelley Tanaka
and David Craig
If you're in Atchison, Kansas, you can even visit where Amelia grew up:
www.ameliaearhartmuseum.org

Amelia Earhart™ is a trademark of Amy Kleppner, as heir to the
Estate of Muriel Morrissey, www.AmeliaEarhart.com

First published in the UK in 2016 by Frances Lincoln Children's Books,
74–77 White Lion Street, London N1 9PF, UK
QuartoKnows.com
Visit our blogs at QuartoKnows.com

Text copyright © 2016 by Mª Isabel Sánchez Vegara
Illustrations copyright © 2016 by Mariadiamantes

First published in Spain in 2016 under the title *Pequeña & Grande Amelia Earhart*
by Alba Editorial, s.l.u.
Baixada de Sant Miquel, 1, 08002 Barcelona
www.albaeditorial.es

All rights reserved.

Translation rights arranged by IMC Agència Literària, SL

A catalogue record for this book is available from the British Library.

UK ISBN 978-1-84780-885-1

Manufactured in Guangdong, China TT052018

10

Photographic acknowledgements (pages 28-29, from left to right) 1. American aviator Amelia Earhart as a young girl, 1904 © FPG,
Getty Images 2. Amelia Earhart in 1928 © CORBIS 3. Amelia Earhart arrives back in US in 1932 © CORBIS 4. Amelia Earhart's
record-breaking hop over Golden Gate Bridge in 1937 © CORBIS

Also in the *Little People*, **BIG DREAMS** series:

FRIDA KAHLO

ISBN: 978-1-84780-770-0

Meet Frida Kahlo, one of the best artists of the twentieth century.

COCO CHANEL

ISBN: 978-1-84780-771-7

Discover the life of Coco Chanel, the famous fashion designer.

MAYA ANGELOU

ISBN: 978-1-84780-890-5

Read about Maya Angelou – one of the world's most beloved writers.

AGATHA CHRISTIE

ISBN: 978-1-84780-959-9

Meet the queen of the imaginative mystery – Agatha Christie.

MARIE CURIE

ISBN: 978-1-84780-961-2

Be introduced to Marie Curie, the Nobel Prize-winning scientist.

ROSA PARKS

ISBN: 978-1-78603-017-7

Discover the life of Rosa Parks, the first lady of the civil rights movement.

EMMELINE PANKHURST

ISBN: 978-1-78603-019-1

Meet Emmeline Pankhurst, the suffragette who helped women get the vote.

AUDREY HEPBURN

ISBN: 978-1-78603-052-8

Learn about the iconic actress and humanitarian – Audrey Hepburn.